# CONTENTS

# Action Plan for Great Dads

## GORDON MacDONALD

POCKET GUIDES
Tyndale House Publishers, Inc.
Wheaton, Illinois

Quotes from the Bible are taken from *The Holy Bible*, Revised Standard Version.

*Action Plan for Great Dads* is adapted from *The Effective Father* by Gordon MacDonald © 1977 by Tyndale House Publishers, Inc. Additional material is taken from *Action Guide for Effective Fathers* by Bob Buechner, Pat McMillan, and Jim Webb. Printed by Tyndale House Publishers. © 1979 by Bob Buechner, Pat McMillan, and Jim Webb. Used by permission.

Second printing, July 1988
Library of Congress Catalog Card Number 86-50593
ISBN 0-8423-0014-7
© 1986 by Gordon MacDonald
All rights reserved
Printed in the United States of America

# *What Makes a Great Dad?*

Someone asks for a definition of family leadership. They want something in twenty-five words or less—and I struggle to deliver.

Finally I shoot back, "Define for me a quarterback. Where do you begin? With leadership charisma? Snap decision-making ability? Fast eyes? Strong arm? Capacity to scramble? Or how about a legal description: his position on the field, the limits in which he can move, and the things he can and cannot do? Twenty-five hundred words maybe!"

## ORDERING THE HOME

Perhaps the place to begin a definition of leadership in the home is with the recognition that we need order in family relationships. People living in proximity to one another must follow some pattern of relationship or there will be conflict and chaos. I believe God has chosen one person in a family—the father—to create and maintain the needed order. There is both a positive and negative side to his role.

*On the positive side,* a father's leadership is designed to bring people to maturity, to the greatest reaches of their human potential. A leader searches out the conditions in which each person in his family can grow to be what God meant him or her to be.

*On the negative side,* a father's leadership is the enforcement of order when someone is unwilling to fit into the process of relationships. Without correction, one person's attitude can make life miserable for everyone.

The head of the home—like the shepherd in Psalm 23—carries a kind of rod and staff: the staff for rescue and direction, the rod for discipline and enforcement. When both are capably used, there is stability in relationships. When both are unused or misused, there is drift and deterioration among the shepherd's sheep—and the father's family.

## SETTING THE PACE

Most auto racing appears to me to be carnage on wheels. But I must confess to an annual habit of tuning in on Memorial Day to find out who the winner is at Indianapolis.

The race begins with a pace-car, a beautiful new automobile especially chosen each year to get out in front of the high-powered racers and lead them around the track for a few laps. The pace-car guarantees that every race driver receives a fair chance, that everyone is in his proper position and moving at a uniform speed when the green starting flag is dropped. At the moment the pack of race cars is properly positioned, the pacer gets out of the way—fast.

Childhood can be likened to that period when the race cars follow the pace-car around the track. Families need a great dad not only because young individuals need order, but because they desperately need to be prepared for the day when the serious race of life is on.

Without the pace-car, you would have confusion. Without a father who takes the lead, a family struggles.


## PATTERNS FOR LEADERSHIP

When I see great fathers in action, I am impressed with how many different ways there are to create order in the home and set the pace for family growth. No one pattern stands out from all the others. Each pattern fits the man.

But despite the differences, I see some common elements—consistent ways in which the lives of children must be touched. A great dad:

- recognizes his enemies
- communicates effectively
- makes himself available
- sets clear precedents

- exercises foresight
- establishes rules for home life
- weighs his decisions.

Each of these practices deserves our scrutiny.

# *Counter Your Competition*

I'll never forget the Saturday morning our son, Mark, was born. As I looked at his tiny body for the first time, it was impossible for me to believe that his life could actually be a prize over which various forces might fight for influence.

I had stayed at my wife's side through the natural delivery, and both of us had witnessed life's most spectacular event—the birth of a child. From Gail's body had emerged a healthy boy, and the two of us could not have felt more satisfaction—Gail, that she had witnessed the birth; and I, that I had not fainted in the delivery room!

Leaving the hospital an hour later to begin the long-distance calls to scattered family members, I brooded about the mysterious business of being a father. I was little more than a boy myself; what could I know about the demands of fatherhood? And how could I imagine the fads, philosophies, and varieties of hucksters and widget salesmen who would attempt to seduce Mark away

from me and the style of life I desired for
him?

## THE BEGINNINGS OF BATTLE
During his first two years of life we encoun-
tered little outside interference; Mark was
all ours. The few outsiders who spent time
with our son were handpicked by his mother
or myself. It was no problem to provide a
home where, like the one on the range, "sel-
dom was heard a discouraging word" or, for
that matter, any kind of word that was abu-
sive or destructive.

To be sure, there were early parent-child
struggles, but they were the typical ones:
matters of respect for authority and prop-
erty, obedience, potty-training, and truth-
telling. We generally succeeded in setting
patterns for relationships with which we
were comfortable. I naively concluded that
this challenge of being a father wasn't so
formidable after all.

Then came the "blitzkrieg." It smashed
into our family, targeted right at our son
with the onset of neighborhood friends,
school, television, and the values of a society
that has more money and things than it
knows how to use. By the time Mark was
five, I was a father with battle scars.

## MISTAKES FATHERS MAKE
1. *They build walls.* And how do fathers
cope with this onslaught? Some decide that

the best way to face the crippling attacks is to stop the clock. They build walls around their families or make cloisters of their communities. All progress is pronounced evil, and new styles of dress, transportation, education, and leisure are stamped unlawful.

This pattern of life may offer protection from something, but I'm convinced that life behind walls is not superior to that in the outside world.

2. *They set rigid rules.* Another common response to outside threats to the family is the creation of unbending rules and rigid disciplines that may be as impenetrable as brick walls. From this perspective virtually everything in the world becomes suspect; there is little joy in anything.

When I see people who have a rule book as thick as the phone book, I am reminded of the days of my childhood when my mother would take me into the children's department at Macy's. Just as I was set to launch my lustful promenade among the toys, my mother would sternly remind me: "Don't touch anything!" For children who live in a family where everything is oriented about rules, where everything is treated with a "don't touch," living in the world is a lot like my experience in the toy store. Just look and yearn, but don't touch; never enjoy!

3. *They relax discipline.* The opposite extreme may be just as dangerous—a father who treats life in the world as if there were no evil. His permissive attitude sees no threats, levels no warnings, and expects no

adverse consequences. "I want my children to have every opportunity there is," a father says. "Let them choose the beliefs and styles of life that best suit them."

Somewhere between too much and too little control is a perspective that makes sense. Naturally, civilization isn't all evil, and the amount of reality in the world to discover and enjoy is mind-boggling. But the father who hasn't perceived that life is much like crossing a mine field had better prepare himself for some heavy casualties.

## HOW TO DETECT DANGER

I recall seeing somewhere a war photograph showing a squad of men crossing a heavily mined field. At the point is a specialist carrying a mine detector. Some of the land is apparently safe, but other parts are salted with a lethal punch. Follow the leader, the photo says, and you will stay alive.

Like the mine specialist, a great dad trains his eye to discriminate between things that will build and things that will destroy his children's lives. He begins to notice repetitive hostile patterns in various areas of life—patterns that demand acute, sensitive awareness. He knows that without proper attention, destructive elements may emerge to erode and tear at his children's spirits.

## MINE 1: A MEDIA MINDSET

An internal mine detector might register a

few things capable of exploding in a family's face. For example, it takes an enormous amount of wisdom even to read the daily newspaper. Since the publisher has to print items that appeal to the majority of his readers, some columns tend to include large doses of trivial gossip. More frequently than not, the daily paper includes interviews and descriptions of men and women that are quite shocking.

For example, a mainline article highlighted a New York society woman who claimed to have a happy marriage in which outside affairs were fully known and approved of by her husband. He apparently enjoyed reciprocal privileges. The article is written in amoral terms, passing no judgment—perhaps even implying that if everyone could try it, we would all be emotionally much more healthy.

In fact, fidelity is equated with being uptight. Hardly a week passes without some details about a Hollywood couple living together, raising children outside of marriage, and suggesting that others ought to try it.

Sexual morality is not the only area in which the newspaper sets a tone that says, "Everybody's doing it; what's wrong with me?" The sports pages are constantly filled with vicious criticism of athletes who may have performed poorly on the field the day before or upon a coach who is to be made scapegoat for a losing streak. As a result, human beings are torn apart.

We can't underestimate the insidious effect upon young people who are spectators to words that tear men to shreds, and on the other hand, lionize them when they break rules and escape the consequences. The whole mentality says something to the young family member who learns a new way of thinking and evaluation. Turn to the editorial pages; the same mind-set persists, only the attacks there zero in on politicians, educators, and religious leaders.

Television picks up where the newspaper leaves off and amplifies it all in living color. Suggestive situation comedies are but one example of a shallow view of human commitment. Soap operas describe a trail of broken and twisted relationships; game shows communicate the idea that material objects are infinitely desirable and can be acquired easily; violence of every kind tends to anesthetize our children—and ourselves—to the horror of actual suffering and death.

These are some of the ways the electronic and printed media create a battlefield upon which the' effective father must fight. The answer does not lie in canceling the papers or banning the TV. That's been tried, and it doesn't work. The only answer is awareness and active participation in evaluating the alternatives and choosing healthy media input. What father who loves his family would permit just any unknown person to enter his home freely? In this age of communications his job as doorkeeper extends to those who enter through print and airwaves.

## MINE 2: JOB DEMANDS

Many fathers face a struggle with the world of industry. I call it the problem of the absent dad. He is what the term implies: gone too much. We can't turn the clock back, but a quick glance at the typical father in the agricultural era might help us to see the mess we're in.

The farm family worked together, and the father was on display for all to see. Children not only saw their dad resting in the evening, if he got a chance, but they saw him performing under pressure and stress. If the cow kicked over a pail of milk, the kids were probably on hand to assess Dad's response. If a hailstorm wiped out the crop, they shared his grief. They were with him during the birth, care and feeding, and death of animals.

It was this constant family fellowship that molded the life-style of each child. But that constant presence simply doesn't exist any longer in most families. Since a father leaves home in the early morning hours, his productive role in the world, his personal reactions under stress, his most meaningful relationships are all hidden from his children. In those times when they could have learned most, he is absent from them. The end of the day is usually marked by fatigue and staleness.

In this new system of life that we have arranged for ourselves, intergenerational work rarely exists. Home life tends to be leisure-oriented—home is the place where we all come to relax, eat, and sleep. The center for creativity and productivity has been transferred from the home to the office, the school, and the marketplace.

The absent dad creates high-voltage tension in the home, forcing mothers to assume responsibilities that should not be theirs, and denying children the kind of exposure to their fathers that they desperately need.

## MINE 3: PEER GROUP PRESSURES

Even when parents are present and involved with their children, the family structure can be seriously jeopardized by the children's peers.

The structure of our society has isolated people by age groups for large blocks of time each day. The adolescent, for example, is separated from younger people and thus can lose the chance to develop responsibility. He has little contact—except on an adversary basis—with most adults. His interest is forced to the horizontal—to those who are his age. With them he finds a kind of fulfillment, a shared feeling of parental oppression. Popularity becomes an issue based on frighteningly superficial criteria.

Due to the peer structure, entire age-oriented cultures emerge, identified by dress styles, special vocabularies, and unique kinds of social protocol. Industries have grown up appealing to the tastes of peer cultures. Radio stations direct a format at one particular age grouping.

The stronger the horizontal relationships, the weaker the vertical family unit. The two cannot peacefully coexist. More than one family has coasted along with what the parents thought were good relationships until a child or two reached middle adolescence. Suddenly—sometimes within weeks—breaks in communication occurred, new loyalties appeared, and a father and mother found themselves bewildered. What happened?

## HOW'S YOUR HOME LIFE?

Rate the following items in terms of their negative impact in your home.

| | No Danger | | | Increasing Danger | | | | | | Crisis |
|---|---|---|---|---|---|---|---|---|---|---|
| | 1 | 2 | 3 | 4 | 5 | 6 | 7 | 8 | 9 | 10 |
| Newspapers/ magazines | | | | | | | | | | |
| Books | | | | | | | | | | |
| Television/ movies | | | | | | | | | | |
| Music | | | | | | | | | | |
| My schedule | | | | | | | | | | |
| My child's schedule | | | | | | | | | | |
| Affluence | | | | | | | | | | |
| Peer group pressure | | | | | | | | | | |

"Would you believe that we never had an ounce of trouble with her?" a mother says. "Then September came and she started the ninth grade. I don't think it was more than a couple of weeks until we noticed a change in her dress, the way she spoke to her younger brother, and the kind of boys she admired. Every discussion degenerated into an argument; every weekend became a crisis over where she wanted to go and with whom. She just wore her father and me down. It was as if we were suddenly living with a different person."

The description is not a rare one. Peer culture can have a powerfully divisive effect.

---

## A Father's Resolve

The stakes are high. Arrayed against me are those who wish to extract money, loyalty, and the strong creative energy my son or daughter may have to give. In the eternal dimension, the prize is the soul of my children.

I am not prepared to compromise or negotiate. Until my children are old and wise enough to distinguish their enemies from their friends, I hold the responsibility to conduct both a defense and an offense on their behalf, demonstrating all the time how and why it is done for their benefit.

# Talk Straight

Words have an awesome impact. They can build or they can destroy. The impressions made by a dad's voice can affect the course of a life. He has the opportunity to choose his words, but he cannot always control the consequences that his words create.

If a father is prone to lose his temper and pour out uncontrolled words, he may find himself living with a crushed son or daughter. Words that explode at an impressionable moment can shape an entire personality.

## WORDS THAT WORK

A father initiates action in his family through words, and he motivates continuous action through words. He tells his children what he wishes them to be, to learn, or to do.

The idea is not for a father to sit like a sultan, giving orders that maintain his own comfort and leisure. Rather, a great dad assumes the role of family manager, using his

# Tom's Story

A forty-two-year-old man has allowed me to look into the inner recesses of his life and see what makes him what he is today: a man who is frantically working himself into exhaustion; one who spends every dime he makes for impressive artifacts of luxury and success; a volatile human being whose temper explodes at the slightest hint of disagreement or criticism.

At one impressionable point in boyhood, when my friend was apparently displeasing his father with the way he was doing a chore, his father said to him, "Tom, you will always be a bum. You're not going to amount to a thing; you're a bum!" Tom goes on to tell me that whenever he and his father had angry moments, the same prediction would be repeated until it burned its way into the boy's spirit like shrapnel embedded in flesh.

Thirty years later, Tom still suffers from his father's verbal abuse. The words drive him day and night to a subconscious attempt to prove that his father was wrong. Ironically, even though Tom's father is dead, the habit patterns of Tom's inner life still maintain fever pitch to convince a dead father and a slightly unsure Tom that he is not a bum. Let anyone suggest to Tom that he is doing something wrong or that he is deficient in some way, and his hostility, defensiveness, and furious energy are unleashed against the old accusations from a thoughtless father who verbally set a wrong pace.

perspective to bring the family experience to a level of productivity and maturity. When he talks with his children, he must keep the ground rules of effective verbal communication.

## TALK WITH CLARITY

Talking with children demands a heavy-duty effort at verbal clarity. Somehow Dad has to find the words that convey to his kids exactly what he wants to say. If they do not understand him, their responses are going to be out of line with what he had in mind.

Compare the subtle difference between these three statements when a father is trying to initiate action:

- "I want you to be in bed by nine o'clock."
- "I think you should be in bed by nine o'clock."
- "I'd appreciate it if you were in bed by nine o'clock."

A discerning father knows exactly which of these phrases will activate which children. The younger the child, the more direct the words need to be. The more mature the child, the softer the direction-giving.

Eventually, of course, the time comes when the habit pattern is established and there need be no instruction at all. Instructions properly given to children result in habits rightly implemented by adolescents.

## SET TIME LIMITS

A time limit is also important for young children, and it's part of the ground rules. Time, like words, means different things to different people. Time moves slowly for a child; it flies for an adult. Forgetting this, it is easy for a father to expect his children to regard the value of time just as he does. But in fact they do not.

When Mark and Kris were between three and four years of age we began to give them daily chores as part of family life. They were capable of emptying wastebaskets, straightening towels in the bathroom, and putting all of their personal things in their place.

The problem we had was not with clarity of directions; it was with certain time limits. Chores were to be done before breakfast. But because the children would sometimes be slower than usual, breakfast was put off later and later while we all but lost our patience trying to get the kids to finish their jobs.

The timer on the stove solved our problem. I gathered the kids together. I informed them that I was through raising my voice in order to scare them into action. Each morning, I said, the timer would be set for thirty minutes. When it reached the zero mark and the bell sounded, job-time was over.

During the half hour I was not going to speak about jobs at all. At the zero mark we would sit down to eat. The timer was the judge; if the work was not complete, there would be a consequence: possibly an earlier bedtime at the end of the day.

I never had to interpret time and deadline again. The stove timer took care of everything. The clock was ruthless, and the kids discovered they could not ask it to be lenient or to slow down to accommodate their mood.


## SPEAK WITH CERTAINTY

Another ground rule fathers often violate is certainty of command. Are the sounds a father makes certain or uncertain?

Children become astute—outdone only by their older brothers and sisters—at making accurate assessments as to how much their father means when he says something. In the life of an average dad there are a lot of uncertain sounds—enormous differences between his words and his actual intentions.

"John, I want you to go to bed," a father says. John grunts but does not move. Four minutes later: "John, I told you to go to bed." John's grunt now turns into English: "All right, Dad." But this is a stalling tactic worked to perfection after years of experience. John hardly even breaks rhythm with what he is doing. He knows the certain sound has yet to come. Everything so far is uncertain, actually inoperative.

"John," (the voice of John's father is now raised several decibels in volume) "I said get to bed." John now moves toward the bedroom. Why? Because John responds to noise levels, not words.

In John's home, volume is the scale of seriousness. Soft sounds are uncertain; loud ones mean business. If John is bold enough, he may have the temerity to say as he retires, "All right, you don't have to yell at me." But he knows and acts in a way that proves his father does have to yell. That is the system of command John's father has inadvertently created.

### The Sounds of Certainty

- You mean what you say.
- You make the request once.
- You count to ten.
- You don't raise your voice.
- You don't repeat what you are sure was heard the first time.

## REBUKE WITH GENTLENESS

Correction should be done in such a way that it builds or redirects the child.

The Bible calls corrective confrontation a rebuke. A rebuke stands between an ungodly act and its painful consequence. It is the last warning sign that is given when a person is headed in the wrong direction and will end up in the discard pile if he does not stop and turn around.

Fathers sometimes get confused about rebukes. All too often, rebukes are launched out of vengeance and anger. A careful examination of my own rebukes tells me that a large number of them are not designed to build character into the lives of my kids; rather, they are designed to halt certain things that are momentarily inconvenient for me. Since I am bigger than they are, I can make my will supreme. Thus, I may speak sharply or in anger because I am irritable, or I am tired, or because I want some peace for myself. In fact, my rebukes may not be rebukes at all; they may simply be adult temper tantrums.

A ten-year-old boy dissects an old alarm clock in his father's shop. When Dad arrives home that night, he discovers his work bench littered with tools and alarm clock parts. Finding his son downstairs, he explodes, "Son, I'm sick and tired of finding my shop in such a mess when I come home at night. You're not responsible about these things; you're messy and you never finish anything. Don't you realize how expensive these tools are?" A series of outbursts like that may stifle the boy's curiosity, his desire to work in the shop, or his hunger to enter this aspect of his father's world at all.

It could be made into a teachable moment, engendered through gentle rebuke. "Son, I'm delighted that you have had time to take a clock apart today. I'm anxious to hear what you learned about the clock. But what would you do if you had to use these tools right away for another job?

"Now I'm excited to see you getting into

something like this, and you know that most of the tools are there for you to use. But part of the way we do things here in the shop is never to use something without putting it back. In fact, the job isn't done until all the tools are put away. Why don't you tell me what you did with the clock while you clean things up. I'll stay here with you until the job is done."

Curiosity is affirmed; the father's pleasure in the boy's interest in tools is highlighted; and the necessary lesson is learned. That's a gentle rebuke, and it is sure to build the boy's life.


TWO WAYS TO SET THINGS STRAIGHT
There is a part of every one of us that resists authority as long as possible. Children will shift from dead-center obedience just as long as a lazy father allows them to. Therefore a great dad is always evaluating the time it takes to get a response from a clearcut signal. When he senses drift, he must immediately retune the relationship.

1. *Call a family meeting.* "Children," a father says, "I have become increasingly aware that you are putting your mother and me off when we speak to you about something. You really don't give us your attention until we've shouted or given several warnings. I can't accept that! I don't plan to keep on shouting or repeating myself, and I know your mother doesn't either. I'm sure that you don't care for it anymore than we do.

So because we all probably agree on that, I'm going to suggest that we go back to the first-time system. I'm going to say a thing once; if I'm sure you've heard and understood, I won't repeat myself. If I see that there's no reaction to what I've said, there will be a consequence. Now do you all understand what I'm planning for us to do? Kevin, tell me what you think I've just said."

The first-time system is implemented, and when a test-case arrives—as it will— Dad performs just as he promised. Consequence! You can be sure that the family will be watching from the next room to see if their dad meant what he said.

2. *Follow through and make sure the children respond.* Leadership in the family is a disaster when fathers do not check out the reactions to their requests and directions. The man who asks his children to play quietly, eat in a more orderly way, wash their hands, or prepare for bed—but overlooks the results when his words are ignored—is really being dishonest. His statements are indications of "wish" rather than "want" for the family's good. It doesn't take a child long to see that his father doesn't mean what he says; he hasn't even bothered to check up on the results of what he's asked.

Is there anyone who hasn't at one time or another seen a father lose control of an unruly child? He keeps telling the child to quiet down, but never reinforces his words with actions. These fathers will wonder in years to come why their children ignore them completely. It will probably never occur to them that the rebellious part of every human being establishes a pattern of listening only to those people who follow through, checking on the results of what they've initiated.

## DO YOU TALK STRAIGHT?
If you wanted your child to obey you, what would you do? Check one of the boxes below.

☐ 1.  I would ask my wife to speak to the child; she's better at this sort of thing than I am.
☐ 2.  I would remind my child of the consequences of disobeying me.
☐ 3.  I don't need to threaten my child; he already knows how angry I'll be if he disobeys.
☐ 4.  I would tell my child exactly what I would like him to do and give him a deadline for doing it.

The best answer to the above question is number four. If you gave another answer, reread pages 19 to 27 carefully.


## THREE MODELS TO AVOID
1. *The threatening father.* The father who issues threats thinks he is giving directions, but he unwittingly gives choices instead. And they are usually prefaced with the word *if:* "If you don't turn off the TV and get to your homework, I'll take the TV away for the next two days," he says.

He doesn't know it, but he has confronted his child with a calculated decision. Experience may suggest that there is a fifty-fifty chance of Dad remembering his threat to-morrow; he'll probably be away on business anyway. "I'll risk it," a child decides uncon-sciously, and he proceeds on a status quo basis.

Father never thought of his directive as a choice; he saw the second part of his state-ment as a possible consequence. But his child saw it as an alternative. Threats are usually bluffs, and the shrewd child reads them as a pro quarterback reads defenses. To put it another way, he can calculate the odds of the threatened consequence better than Jimmy the Greek.

There will be times when a child will ac-cept the consequences of the threat. This will become particularly true as the son or daughter grows older. A typical threat—"If you're not home by 11:30 P.M., you'll be grounded for two weeks"—may turn into a choice at 11:15 P.M. when the teenager is having so much fun that the promise of a two-week suspension is worth the gamble. At 12:15, when the homecoming happens, Dad is faced with implementing a conse-quence he would prefer to avoid—especially if the next two weeks include some activities he wanted his son or daughter to experi-ence.

2. *The exploding father.* This dad doesn't understand the ground rules of response either. He just blows up, spewing words in every direction. He's inconvenienced, embarrassed, or simply feels defeated be-

cause—to use the words of one TV comedian—he "don't get no respect."

I overheard two boys talking the other day. One asked the other, "What's your old man going to say when Mr. Amsden tells him that you cut class?" The second responded, "Oh, he'll get mad and tell me off, but he'll get over it pretty quick. I'm not too worried about him."

Some children are worried. They reflect their concern with statements like, "My folks are going to kill me when they hear about this." But the attention has been mistakenly centered on the explosion, not the building process.

It is sad to analyze these exchanges between young people and realize that what they're saying is that ineffective fathers have temper tantrums, little else. They are saying that if you can devise a way to weather the parental storm, you can pretty much get anything you really want. The exploding father isn't really building human beings; he's simply causing a mild inconvenience to a child who is learning how to do exactly what he wants to do. He's telling his kids that he doesn't like what they're doing, but if they can stand the heat, it won't matter much what he likes or doesn't like.

3. *The silent father.* This dad says nothing. If we could bring deficient fathers into court under charges of neglect in home leadership, the silent father would face the sternest charges.

A woman talked with me about her husband who is an athletic coach. On the playing field he is a man with superhuman capacities, running back and forth, urging his players with a booming voice, forcefully correcting their tiniest imperfections. He can affirm them with an enthusiasm heard for blocks.

His wife sobbed as she described his homecoming each evening. An exhausted, almost depressed man makes his way through the door, flops on the couch with the evening newspaper, and is asleep within minutes. He rises only for supper, returning to the couch for an evening of television and beer-drinking. His personality takes on color only if friends who know something about sports come to visit, or if the assistant coaches and players drop by for a skull session on next week's game. In the meantime, three children are growing up, and he takes little interest in them. He is a sensational coach, but a silent father.

My friend the silent dad may understand the ground rules on the athletic field, but he doesn't know the rules in his home. He wouldn't be impressed at all if I warned him that he was laying a foundation for his children to hate sports, hate rules, hate men, and even hate him.

# *Check Your Approachability*

He was a tiny tot in a cartoon, and everywhere he turned to find some attention in the family, he got the polite brush-off. Mother was too busy; Dad was preoccupied. In frustration he finally gave up. Looking straight out at the reader, he analyzed the family situation this way: "The story of my life is a busy signal."

Busy signals on the telephone rank near the top of my own personal list of ordinary, everyday irritants. That pulsating tone that fills the ear always seems to be an insult, and although I try hard not to, I sometimes take it personally that someone is not eagerly awaiting my call—and my call alone.

## BUSY SIGNALS IN THE HOME

Children, too, hear frequent busy signals. No home is without some of them, of course. But we live in a day when children are confronted with far too many messages from their fathers—messages that amount to "Don't bother me! I'm tied up!"

I am reminded of this when I sit next to a mother and father at PTA who, in the more boring moments of the evening, fill out a summer camp application for their three children. They are preparing to spend six hundred dollars each week for seven weeks in order to relieve themselves of the kids for the summer. An expensive busy signal!

Most destructive busy signals occur right in the home. Some begin with the words, "Not now; later . . ." Variations on that theme can be seen in the following phrases: "Wait until your dad finishes the . . ." or "Can't you find something else to do?" or "Ask your mother" or "Son, Dad's awfully tired right now." When I researched the effect of these responses on my inquiring children, I discovered I didn't even have to leave my home to feel distance between us.

## WHY WE TUNE OUT OUR KIDS

Why do we frequently find ourselves irritated, hold ourselves aloof, give busy signals when our children try to reach out and touch us? There are several possibilities.

1. *We don't want to upset our schedules.* A child's needs appear to be so impulsive—so unplanned in contrast to our more ordered way of living. We've looked forward to a quiet evening in front of the fireplace, and what's more, the anticipation has sustained us all day. But the children haven't had this dream; they wish to play a game. We've been planning to spend the evening finishing off the income tax forms, but one of the kids needs help on a science project.

Fresh in my own mind are countless struggles I have when my carefully planned schedule is endangered by the demands of my children. They seem to enjoy having me around, so they plot a daily plan for my life. They want to talk and share with me all sorts of "interesting" things that are on their minds. They want to include me in their games. They expect me to drop everything and sit down with them in front of the television. When I protest and try to beg off, Gail will devastate my defenses with a remark like, "Don't worry, honey; in just a few years they won't bother you at all. In fact, they won't even want you around." So I give in and talk, play, or watch TV with them.

2. *We have trained ourselves to listen only to those things we feel are important.* Since the interests of children are less than important in the eyes of adults, we are tempted not to listen to them. Children do not have information that earns money; they don't know influential people; and they do not normally have insights or new ideas that will change our world. We'll listen to them later . . . when they grow up.

But why, then, don't our children understand that our busy signals are only temporary? Why do they begin to "dial" other numbers as they grow older? There are a lot of fathers of teenagers asking that kind of question today.

We forget what we convey through our busy signals. If a daughter comes into a living room night after night with a question, only to be cut off with "Dear, wait until I finish the paper and then I'll talk with you," she will hear a more cruel translation than the surface meaning of the words. She hears, "You're not as important as the paper is; you will always be relatively unimportant."

3. *We would rather speak.* Sometimes we feel that what we have to say is more important than what we have to hear. There may be an ironic tragedy to that gross misunderstanding, because the man who does not know how to listen will not really know what to say.

## Children: Seen *and* Heard

The children of my generation were often told that "children should be seen and not heard." So as youngsters we concluded that virtuous behavior was to sit quietly while adults talked. The implication was that nothing that came out of a child's mouth was of any significance.

Fortunately, God does not believe in that dictum. Every child, God says, is important. And what's more, everything a child says will be heard; the line to heaven is open. Perhaps, after it has been heard, it will receive a rebuke, a correction, or even a retribution—but it will be heard.

4. *We don't know how to listen.* A young father, trying very hard to be honest about his problems with his wife and children, says to me, "Frankly, I'm not a sensitive man. I am constantly discovering that my family is telling me things about themselves and their needs, and I am not hearing them. I completely miss the points they are trying to make. What am I doing wrong?"

As I talk to him and his wife, I notice immediately how far apart they are in their methods of communication. He attacks her words as a theologian might exegete a Greek phrase. But in the few minutes I am with them, I am already aware that she communicates in tones of voice, pauses, facial expressions, and gestures. But he is missing all of this, and thus missing her real message. No one has ever taught him how to listen. If he cannot even understand his wife, his misunderstanding of his children must be immense.

A great dad deliberately develops a facility to listen to his family—to hear what is being said, and sometimes to hear what is not being said. He has finely tuned his open ear to hear:

- tones of voice
- certain kinds of silence and broodishness
- special styles of crying
- code words that imply frustration, heartbreak, or rebellion
- pained looks of distress
- slumping postures of personal defeat and discouragement.

He hears the signals and interprets them correctly.


YOUR CHILD'S NEEDS
What is it that children want when they approach their fathers? What are they looking for?

*Answers to questions.* A great dad will listen for questions, the answers to which will shape a child's mind and spirit.

It is rush hour and the traffic is snarled beyond description. A voice comes from the backseat, "Daddy, what does God look like?" With a question like that, it is no time to throw out a busy signal. Traffic jams aren't going to stop you from conversation one bit.

*Affection and physical tenderness.* A child turns moody and seemingly disrespectful at the dinner table. A father's impulse might be to strongly reprimand the child and perhaps even to punish him. But sensing the behavior is a bit out of character, the father suggests that the two go to the child's bedroom for a few minutes.

"Son, your behavior at the table was unacceptable. Now if you're just testing me to see how far I'll go, I'm ready to do something about it . . . now! But if you're telling me that something is really bothering you that I don't know about, I'd like you to share it with me."

The child dissolves into tears, and piece by piece the feelings emerge. During the past few days it seems as if every judgment call in the house has gone against him. He feels alone.

The father realizes in a moment that it just may seem like that. He draws the boy to himself and holds him quietly and lovingly for ten minutes while the child sobs out his pent-up feelings of frustration and futility. In the hugging and touching is reaffirmation. This was not a time for punishment, and the listening father caught the real message— just in time.

*Attention to feelings of inadequacy.* The child who constantly pesters his parents throughout an evening may really be saying, "I have to keep on testing you to know if you really think I'm worthwhile and important."

A daughter becomes irritating because she keeps wanting to climb on her father's lap and be affectionate. He keeps giving her busy signals, and she keeps persisting. But if he should stop everything for just a few minutes and give her the attention she seeks, he may discover that her interest quickly subsides. She has found out what she needed to know; she's important to him.

A boy keeps downgrading himself when it comes to his ability to read. He claims he doesn't enjoy it, that he gets nothing out of it, that there are no good books, anyway. What he may really be saying is that he's not sure that he's a very good student. An hour spent with his father reading together just may turn the tide in another direction.

*Companionship.* "Dad, would you go up to the store with me?" "Dad, would you drive for the Cub Scouts' field trip next week?" "Dad, would you sit here for a few minutes while I go to sleep?" These are no times for busy signals.


PRIME TIME WITH DAD

The very best of us will sometimes make mistakes in this business of listening. For example, I misread my son one evening when I was preparing to take a houseguest to the airport for his return home. Before we left, I turned to Mark and suggested that he go along. He immediately accepted.

As we were getting our coats on, I issued the same invitation to our daughter, Kris. Out of the corner of my eye, I noticed a cloud come over Mark's face. Not reading the signals correctly, I thought I saw pure selfishness. I was sure I was right when throughout the ride to and from the airport, Mark remained absolutely silent, almost physically turning away whenever his sister spoke either to him or to me.

When we returned home, I sent Kris into the house and began to lecture him; first, for being so selfish, and second, for pouting when things did not go his way.

The full story came later. When I pieced things together, I found that I had misinterpreted his signals. I discovered that his disappointment was based on the fact that he needed to discuss some things alone with me. His mind had been preoccupied with some special challenges he was facing on his soccer team and he was uneasy about them. He believed that talking with me about them might help him to meet them. I had not sensed that. Not having "heard," I gave him a busy signal.

It would be hard to do an instant replay of that whole affair and find out how I could have done a better job. But it stands as an example of how a father can totally misread a child's mind. I should have seen red flags at the beginning, but I didn't. I assumed peevishness when I should have heard honest disappointment. Not attuned to the fact that it had been several days since he had been alone with me, I blew a chance to provide a few intimate moments.

As a result of that experience, I learned there are times when my children are not content to be simply part of a group, even a family group. They want and deserve prime time with Dad—alone. I listen for those times now.

### When to Listen to Your Kids
- At bedtime
- In times of sickness
- After successes—and failures
- During vacations
- During special outings

## LISTENING WITH ACCEPTANCE

A great dad needs to develop a quality I call unconditional acceptance. Children and teenagers are far more prone to engage in dialogue with a father who accepts them as persons, placing no conditions upon the relationship.

Long hair, loud music, and a host of other symbols of the younger generation have split more fathers from their children than can be imagined. I have met fathers who can never quite get beyond the appearance of their sons in order to have an intelligent discussion about real issues.

Among the many things fathers wish from their children are emulation, respect, and agreement. It may bother us when a child begins to prefer a model of car other than the one we think is the best. As the years pass, we may make the painful discovery that their understanding of success is different than ours.

---

## Making Time to Listen

A businessman I know resigned his job and moved from a prestigious suburb. He now runs a quiet bakery business which keeps him busy, to be sure, but gives him large blocks of time to enjoy his family. I asked him why he had made such a decision. He recalled for me a day when he and his wife and two children were driving in the car. The boy had asked his mother the final score of a certain basketball game.

"I suddenly realized it was the kind of question a son usually asks his father, not his mother. I was hit with the awareness that I'm gone so much of the time that the children have gotten used to addressing all their questions to their mother."

That painful observation caused one man to change his life-style. He now enjoys having time to listen to his children.

Each of these and many other discoveries set off uneasy vibrations within us. We mistake independent thought for rejection and even rebellion. If we are not careful, conversations tend to concentrate on surface issues. We begin to make it plain that we are disappointed, even embarrassed, over their style and evaluation of life.

No book on fatherhood could ever hope to present a formula for knowing how much independence a child should have from the value systems of his parents. Perhaps the answer lies not in formulas, but in prayerful wisdom.

A friend who fathered three handsome teenage boys, all of whom wore their hair in the long style, told me how he approached what he thought was a problem. He sat his sons down and leveled with them. "Boys, your choice of hairstyle turns men in my generation off. But it apparently turns the men in your generation on, and I'll accept that. If you wear your hair long because that's the prevailing style, fine. But if it is a symbol of rebellion against your father while you live in our home, then I'll wrestle each of you to the floor and cut it off myself."

The sons assured their father of their respect and love for him, and aside from good-natured kidding, the issue was never mentioned again. Perhaps that's why the sons try to get home to their parents every chance they can, now that they live in other parts of the world. They're accepted for what they are—not for what they look like.

**WHAT'S YOUR ACCEPTANCE QUOTIENT?**
Is there something about the way your child *looks* that you have difficulty accepting? The way he *thinks* about certain issues? The way he *acts* in certain circumstances?

If your answer to any of those questions is yes, how well are you handling your responses?

- ☐ Excellent—from mine and my child's perspective.
- ☐ O.K., with periodic flare-ups.
- ☐ I'm doing all right on the outside, but struggling with a lot of feelings on the inside.
- ☐ Poor on all accounts.

For suggestions, read pages 42 to 47.


## HOW WILL YOU REACT TO WHAT YOU HEAR?

It was the middle of the night when Kris called my name. I heard her first "Daddy!" immediately and sprang out of bed and down the hall to her room. She was in distress. There had been a bad dream, and Kris was having a rough time sorting out what was real and what was part of the dream.

Why had she called her dad? Because her instinct somehow told her that when equilibrium is in jeopardy, fathers can help restore balance. Her young mind had set up a pattern of response to uneasy situations: call for Dad; he knows how to make upside-down things turn right side up again. So in obedience to pattern she called, and I came.

Suppose I had chosen to belittle the

"dumb dream"? Suppose I had yelled down the hall, "What do you want?" and responded with, "Don't worry about it! Everything will be all right; go back to sleep."

What would I really be saying? "Don't dump your problems on me; work them out for yourself. Your feelings are immature and stupid; make them dissolve. But by all means, leave me alone so I can get some sleep."

But I didn't do that; I have learned that response to my children when they are in crucial moments is of utmost importance.

Through our responses we often set into concrete exactly what our children will become. *We are the most important people in the world to them* for a number of years. Our opinions are the ones that count the most. Our responses to their first experimental thrusts of independent personhood will shape their personalities and worldviews in an almost indelible way.

Take self-expression, for example. A child dares to share a poem he has written. Gingerly he brings it to the living room where the family sits. The imagery is crude, the words misspelled, and the thought so naive that to an adult it is really quite amusing. But in sharing his thoughts, the child has actually laid his or her soul out on the carpet. Here is a crisis of response. The child is making a first tentative attempt to reach out of himself and gain affirmation.

The proper response must be praise. Even if the poem is a disaster, the very act of creating it is in itself worthy of enthusiastic applause. But some fathers would dismiss the poem with laughter, and if the laughter is cutting and derisive enough, the child may not take up the pen again.


## WHEN YOUR KIDS BLOW IT

Approachability demands a flexible response, not only in creative moments, but also when things go sour.

Not long ago Gail and I heard the crash of breaking glass come from our living room. Running in the direction of the noise, we found our daughter behind a table where she was trying to retrieve a ball. Her foot had caught a cord, and a lamp—one both her mother and I prize—had fallen over. The globe of the lamp was in several pieces.

Down deep within me was an impulse of immediate anger. I was ready to give vent to the anger because she had been playing ball in an area of the house where ball playing was out of bounds. She deserved—I thought—what my instincts prompted me to deliver.

But on the other hand, one look at her face told me she knew she had been wrong. There she knelt, frozen, awaiting my response. I sensed she was poised on the razor's edge between trusting me with honest repentance or passing the buck. My anger would provoke her to give excuses; my understanding would give rise to her honest evaluation of guilt.

The anger dissolved, and I took her in my arms and hugged her. The tears flowed freely, and she expressed her sorrow. She now understood why we don't play ball games in the living room.

But she understood something even more significant. I am approachable when she has made a bad mistake. In the future when the mistakes are even more dramatic, I want her to remember my response to the broken lamp. I want her to cry out my name instinctively, knowing that I am approachable and will respond in kindness.

The approachability of fathers in the early years of their children's lives will reduce the number of defense mechanisms their children will erect. If they experience sledgehammer reactions in their sour moments, children will develop a remarkable facility for passing responsibility, making excuses, or perhaps taking no risks at all. What father wants that? Much better that the children find in their dads—their great dads—tender responses when their child-sized hearts are faint.

WHY APPROACHABILITY PAYS OFF
Approachability is no simple doctrine of fatherhood to be set forth glibly on paper. We will never adequately fulfill all the demands made upon us by our children; at best, we can only hope to reduce the number of busy signals we send.

But, there is an ironic twist to the doctrine of approachability. The more approachable we are, the more we hasten the day when our children will need to approach us no longer. For as a father listens, accepts, and responds in an affirming manner, he enhances the quality of maturity.

When the children "dial" their father's number, they receive no busy signal. They know he is just a call away. It makes them take greater risks in self-development and acceptance. They grow faster and more wholesomely. And as they mature, they call less and less. They work out their own bad dreams. They develop their own ability to evaluate their creativity. They become independent. But they do so because they know there is a man out there who never responds with a busy signal.

## HOW APPROACHABLE ARE YOU?

How would you evaluate your approachability in the home during an average week? Chart yourself below.

| | | Sun | Mon | Tue | Wed | Thu | Fri | Sat |
|---|---|---|---|---|---|---|---|---|
| Very | 10 | | | | | | | |
| approach- | 9 | | | | | | | |
| able | 8 | | | | | | | |
| | 7 | | | | | | | |
| | 6 | | | | | | | |
| | 5 | | | | | | | |
| | 4 | | | | | | | |
| Not | 3 | | | | | | | |
| approach- | 2 | | | | | | | |
| able | 1 | | | | | | | |

To check your answers, ask your wife and your oldest child to give you separate ratings on the same chart.

# Teach to Build

It is said of Boswell, the famous biographer of Samuel Johnson, that he often referred to a special day in his childhood when his father took him fishing. The day was fixed in his adult mind, and he often reflected upon many of the things his father had taught him in the course of their fishing experience together.

After having heard of that particular excursion so often, it occurred to someone much later to check the journal that Boswell's father kept and determine what had been said about the fishing trip from the parental perspective. Turning to that date, the reader found only one sentence entered: "Gone fishing today with my son; a day wasted."

But no day is ever wasted in the life of a great dad. Few people have heard of Boswell's father; many have heard of Boswell. In spite of his relative obscurity, the elder Boswell must have managed to set a pace in his son's life that lasted for a lifetime. Unknowingly, on one day alone he inlaid along the grain of his son's life ideas that would mark him long into his adulthood. What he did not only touched the boy's life, but set in motion certain benefits that would affect the world of classical literature.


## THE FAMILY CLASSROOM

Family life is a kind of classroom; it lasts for about eighteen years. Each day the effective father stamps into the lives of his children words, attitudes, habits, and responses that one day will become automatic. It would be frightening if a father did not realize this fact. For teach he will—whether he is aware of it or not.

Ironically, teaching can be done either through design or neglect. Teaching, conscious or unconscious, will make an indelible impression upon a child's personality and shape his future character. So the question confronts us: Will we teach to build or teach to cripple?

At this point of discussion, it seems wise to distinguish between abilities and performance and attitudes and values. The first pair are more deliberately taught. The second are often taught by life-style.


## TEACHING YOUR CHILD
## NEW ABILITIES

How does a child discover his or her abilities, gifts, and capacities and put them to work? How can a dad enhance this experience?

1. *Ask your child to assist you.* Think about how many opportunities a father has to ask his children to help him in family responsibilities. For example, a bicycle needs to be repaired. There are at least three ways to approach the need.

- *The lazy father* postpones any action.
- *The busy father* grabs a few minutes, quickly runs the bike into the garage, turns a few screws, and delivers it to his child with the job done.
- *The wise father* adds a few minutes to his schedule and shows his child how to make the repair by sharing the work. His patience may be tested, but the decision will pay off.

A wise dad is perceptive; he knows that several things can be learned in the simple exercise of repairing a bicycle—how to diagnose a problem, select the proper tools, achieve a standard of excellence, bring a job to completion, and clean and maintain tools. For some dads, repairing a bicycle can be an hour wasted; not so for a great dad.

A father shouldn't restrict his teaching about home and engine maintenance to his sons. This is an opportunity for daughters also. We can never foresee the circumstances in which a girl might find herself needing to fix a faulty electric switch, replace a fuse, seat a new faucet washer, change a tire, or jump a faulty solenoid. Nor should a boy be untrained in general work about the house: laundry, cooking, cleaning.

2. *Delegate responsibilities.* Children should be assigned tasks they can reasonably carry through to completion. Actually, it is wise occasionally to give children projects that are just a bit beyond their normal grasp, things that will require mind-exercising and problem-solving. Perceptive fathers may drop a hint now and then, but for the most part, there are times when we should leave our children on their own to surmount obstacles.

There aren't many dads who can master all skills and arts. That's why a man deliberately exposes his children to as many kinds of people as possible. Tours of factories, art studios, business offices, and construction projects have tremendous value. They provide time together, learning experiences, and wholesome recreation. Across the spectrum of activity children begin to sense their own interests. And as they respond with enthusiasm, the discerning father makes a note to delegate—to provide extra amounts of opportunity in that direction.

3. *Encourage good working relationships.* Sharing with children how things are done is not enough. Relationships in the context of work are important also. For example, teaching children the meaning of lines of authority is a significant exercise.

Our twelve- and nine-year-olds decided to

go out on the pond for a canoe ride. As I pushed them off, I reminded both of them that the older one is the captain of the ship; what he says goes. I made sure that both of them understood this important rule of the high seas.

Canoeing has certain dangers. Therefore, I said, it is important that Mark recognize he is in charge. If he says it is time to come in, that is the decision. Kris must accept her brother's authority and appeal to him if she has a certain desire. In the guise of summer fun, a lesson was taught: how to use authority and how to submit to it for the good of the ship and its passengers.

4. *Challenge them with questions.* Driving along with children, a teaching father engages his passengers in conversation with simple "why" questions: "Why do you think they have put all those signs up? Why do you think the builder made the bridge like that?"

"What" questions are also valuable. "What makes that picture attractive? What does that cloud make you think about?"

And add to your bag the "how" questions. "How do you think people will react when they see that load of wrecked cars left in the open field? How do you think we could help that lady who looks sad?"

TEACHING YOUR CHILD
ATTITUDES AND VALUES
Like it or not, a father makes impressions upon his children with far more than his

words. His behavior—the pattern of conduct of his own life—becomes both documentation and justification for anything an offspring wishes to do. More than any other way, a child learns attitudes and values through the life-style of his father.

Children observe. What do they see? The answer separates great dads from the rest of the pack. The great father notes the importance of exposure to his children, realizing that every moment he is with them is a chance for positive character building. The average dad doesn't see this. His view of the family is one of simply living together. For him the home is little more than a meeting place in which to eat, sleep, and have some fun.

When the bulk of a father's time is spent away from the place called home, his model is replaced by the life-styles of school teachers, recreation directors, and child-care personnel. More often than not, children are learning major value systems in life from the horizontal peer culture. The vertical structure is not there in adequate increments of time or intensity to do the job.

Even more tragically, children are finding their life models on the television. The model often chosen and copied is a detective—crude, violent, and amoral. Another model is a foolish caricature in a favorite situation comedy. Worse yet, models arise out of the "free-spirit" personalities of various stars who pride themselves on living beyond the bounds of ordinary restraint.

## WHERE DO YOUR CHILDREN LEARN VALUES?

| | Time<br>Where or with whom do your children spend their time? Estimate your answer in terms of percentages. | Teaching<br>Where or from whom do your children learn? Again, approximate your answer in terms of percentages |
|---|---|---|
| Father | _____________ | _____________ |
| Mother | _____________ | _____________ |
| Father and mother as couple (team) | _____________ | _____________ |
| School | _____________ | _____________ |
| Peer group | _____________ | _____________ |
| Other individuals | _____________ | _____________ |
| Media (TV, magazines, etc.) | _____________ | _____________ |
| Other | _____________ | _____________ |
| Total | 100% | 100% |

## SIX WAYS TO MODEL VALUES

Modeling a life-style demands time and opportunity. Sometimes we have to create experiences that will bring the family together so that learning can take place.

1. *Vacations.* For our family, canoe camping trips are a time for constant exposure. Camping offers a chance to face stress and inconvenience together. We can see each

other in the best and worst circumstances, and we have a chance to test each other's reactions.

To my chagrin, I recall a stormy night in northern Canada when it appeared that our nylon tent might get either blown or washed down the hill. It was miserable. Cold, soaked, and hungry, I performed in less than admirable style. Later I had to apologize to my children for being irritable and snappy. I was angry at something I couldn't control— the weather. Fortunately, there have been other times when my performance out in the bush was better.

Gail and I have often seen the importance of acting calmly for our children under stress at home, when for example, there is an injury and everyone is panic-stricken. That is the time to pray under your breath and assume firm command. These images of action and response are the ones children remember the longest, and they become patterns of how they will act later on.

2. *Games.* Family games—which I generally detest, since I am usually a loser—offer another opportunity for life-style to be modeled. It is important for children to see their parents both win and lose. (At this point, I'd like to give them a chance to see me win. I have no business head for Monopoly; I am unsuccessful at conquering Life; and I always end up with the homely Old Maid.)

Games provide experimental situations in which we can show our behavior under duress, our ability to be honest and considerate, and our attitude toward those who consistently win. A game equalizes everyone under a set of rules. Children climb to the level of their parents on the gameboard while parents descend to the level of children.

3. *Relationships.* Most modeling happens normally in the home each day. In the flow of daily activities the kids are going to see some things which will etch their way into the spirit for future behavior patterns.

Relationships are an important example. Children do not always learn in the schoolroom how to treat one another with dignity and affection. You can't diagram respect, forgiveness, or servanthood. It isn't found in any encyclopedia that I know of. It is observed and then put into motion.

The way in which a father relates to the children's mother is of incalculable significance. The children watch and are strangely warmed when they see Gail and me embrace and kiss. Something tells them that this is a sign of security: all is well in our home. Furthermore, they begin to formulate within their own hearts an understanding of how men treat their wives and how a wife will respond.

My son begins to learn that there are times of the month when a woman needs to be treated with special tenderness and understanding. We may not understand all of her reactions, but he watches and learns from me as he sees me go out of my way to help a bit more conscientiously during those times. And he doesn't fail to note the thankfulness and deepened admiration that is returned from wife to husband. He's learning from the model.

The children also watch us in our conflict. They observe our attempt to pick our way across the prickly field of disagreement, how we choose our words, how we express our disappointment in something the other one has done or thinks. They hear the words "I'm sorry" and "I forgive you," and they learn something about how they should treat other human beings.

It will be obvious that I disagree with those who say all conflicts should be carried on in privacy. Perhaps that is right if there is a marriage where one or both partners cannot control their emotions. But when we face conflict that is always constructive, we can expose ourselves to our children. They need to learn how to exchange differing ideas and perspectives. Where better than from their parents?

## HOW'S MARRIED LIFE?

Rate yourself in the following key areas of your marriage.

| | Dismally Poor | Weak But Improving | Average | Not Bad | Absolutely Outstanding |
|---|---|---|---|---|---|
| Affection | | | | | |
| Conflict | | | | | |
| Work | | | | | |
| Playful | | | | | |
| spontaneity | | | | | |

4. *Work habits.* The way a husband and wife work together is another crucial teaching tool. For a great dad, the old traditions of division of house labor dissolve. A father teaches his sons that no work is intrinsically masculine or feminine. Cleaning kitchens, making beds, helping with housecleaning are all matters that both male and female can and should do. The attitude of the father in this area is of paramount importance.

Also taught through daily routines: the concept of teamwork; the practice of going the extra mile when one senses that another is tired; the need to volunteer to do things over and above normal expectations. These habits inculcate in the spirit of children a realization of the value of productive and helpful labor. And they develop them if they see it first in their father.

The sheer joy of sharing life with other people is also taught in the precedent of a father's life-style. Laughing and enjoying free-spirited kinds of fun are the greatest memories children will carry into the formula of their own relationships. The look on our children's faces the night Gail chased me around the house with an aerosol can of whipping cream was worth a lifetime. The touch football games which always set Mother and Mark against Kris and me, with an ice cream sundae riding on the outcome of the game, are going to make their mark in the children's concept of what joy relationships can reach when we work at them.

5. *Stressful times.* A man's personal per-

formance under stress speaks volumes. I have noted fathers who have an unyielding conviction about churchgoing and religious values, but who can dissolve in unrestrained anger because a neighbor's untreated dandelions blow seed over the fence and onto the front lawn. What about the dad who demands perfect politeness of his children but loses all control of himself when someone cuts him off in a traffic flow? Which behavior pattern speaks louder? Which will be more remembered? Which is more likely to be copied?

We can never overcalculate the intense interest of children when they see their father facing a crisis. How will he act when a flash flood puts six inches of water in the basement? What happens when the misguided hammer hits his thumb? And what of the moment when the umpire wrongly calls him out in the company softball game? Each response under heat of daily living is worth ten thousand verbal statements of personal faith and morality.

6. *Words*. Like actions under stress, words also drive their way home. I think of easy-come-easy-go words a father might use when he evaluates the local police, the governor, or even the highest officers of our country. His tongue may run freely as he expresses his frustration over taxes, crime rates, bureaucracy, and the myriad of common conversations on the subject of government.

"Those dumb police," a father says as he drives along, "always trying to stop speeders with their radar; why don't they spend their time catching the people who are breaking into our homes?" Careless words, spoken in an unguarded moment, fill the child's ears, shaping the attitudes that later will leap to the surface when he has a run-in with the police.

Many homes are filled with unfortunate, critical words about neighbors, close friends, pastors, and other people in significant relationship to us. If parents worry about negative comments and attitudes, it is usually only because they hope that what they have said will not get back to the people who have been the subject of the conversation. But a father's toleration of such critical and negative talk, and, worse yet, his participation in it, simply breeds similar thinking in his children as they grow older. Every word counts.

Wear shoes you want to be filled. The picture of Daddy's little boy clomping down the hall with a pair of his father's shoes on is a nostalgic one. Someday he will do more than simply fill two shoes; he will fill the shoes of a way of life he has seen in his father.

☞ C H E C K P O I N T

Reflect for a moment on your exposure to your children yesterday. What did they observe of your character? Your convictions?

If your actions or behavior from the previous day were actually to be imitated by your children, what would you do differently?

# Find Your Family's Stress Points

Mark was in the bow of our eighteen-foot canoe; I was in the stern. Tied to the thwarts between us was the duffel: tent, sleeping bags, and lots of food.

The river was a boiling white—that is to say, it was running furiously, smashing around and over rocks, here and there climbing up to gunwale-high waves.

We were both paddling downriver, frantically trying to keep afloat through each combination of rapids. Our "survival" depended upon being able to pick a route back and forth across the river that would avoid the ultimate disaster of tipping over and losing everything—especially our pride as great wilderness explorers.

Then it happened! A water-soaked tree lying just below the surface caught the keel of our Grumman canoe and provided the split second the river needed to spin us around. In an instant we were upside down in freezing water, the canoe filled with half

the river. Our equipment could be seen float-
ing downstream.

White water is relentless and unforgiving.
There is only one possible way to beat it,
and that is to keep an eye thirty-five to fifty
yards downriver, anticipating what is ahead.
With foresight, the paddler may manage to
keep dry most of the time.

Something about the instinct of a canoeist
reminds me of family leadership. Life in the
family is like life in white water: the person
steering must always look ahead of the situation. No surprises allowed.

A great dad is foresightful—the very opposite of impulsive. Impulsive fathers usually
find themselves taken by surprise, and that
forces them to act on the spur of the moment. They lose touch with the significance
of circumstances about them; therefore,
they overreact or underreact to many situations.


## THE FATHER WHO
## LACKED FORESIGHT

Take the Bigelow family. John Bigelow's
home is in the full swing of crisis on a Saturday mid-morning. He had planned a family
spring cleanup day, and he had made it plain
that everyone was going to perform some
chores to spruce up the backyard, restore
the garage to order, and repaint fences,
drainpipes, and porch floors.

It was Roger, the ten-year-old, who
brought on the storm. He was irritable,

seemingly lazy, and he griped at every suggestion his father made about the quality and quantity of his work.

Finally, John hit the roof. He called Roger several versions of an ingrate, reminding him of all that the family was always doing to make his life enjoyable. Why, his dad asked, was it so hard for Roger to cheerfully do his part?

Nothing worked! The frustration peaked when Roger was banished to his room for the day. The work accomplished on cleanup day by the rest of the family was now finished in bad humor and out of sheer determination.

Where did it all go wrong? Perhaps—unnoticed by John Bigelow—it began the night before when everyone was out until midnight. The family had been invited to the home of friends, and everyone had gone.

Roger, in the company of other children, had stayed up long after his normal bedtime. Exhilarated by the excitement, he was alert and high when his family reached home after the twelve o'clock hour. He was full of promises for the next day's household activities— promises his youthful emotions and limited physical strength could not keep the next morning.

Roger's father made a strategic mistake when he expected his son to perform at top level the next day. He hadn't thought ahead—"downriver"—when he kept his boy out so late the night before. The next morning his son's reluctance took him by surprise and he showed it in his impulsive anger and unreasonable punishment. Remember, he too had been out late the night before! At no time had Roger's father used foresight.


A foresightful father or an impulsive father—which of these styles of family leadership typically characterizes you? Rate yourself (with an "X") on the following scale.

consistently ___________________ consistently
impulsive          50/50          foresightful

Take a few minutes to discuss the scale with your wife. Where does she rate you?

## COMMON CHILDHOOD PRESSURES

When Mark and I take our Grumman off the top of the car and slip it into the water, we're aware of the potential danger of accidents. We've tried, therefore, to learn the capabilities of our canoe—how it will perform in various situations of wind speed, depth of water, and rate of current.

Knowing the stress-limits of our craft is part of foresightful living on the river.

In the home, family leadership begins

with a father who knows the stress-capacities of his children. This kind of information does not come simply by comparing our children with ourselves as we were at their age. Rather, it comes from studying them and watching them in action. Each one responds to the same circumstances in an entirely different manner. It's especially important to foresee the challenges they face in their trip "downriver" in life.


## INSECURITY

Childhood insecurity arises as the result of uncertain conditions:

- when a child is frequently left with baby-sitters
- when a father travels for long periods of time
- when there is a high level of marital conflict
- when the family moves to another community
- when there is sickness or death in the immediate family.

Adults often underestimate the capacity of small children to sense uneasy situations brewing in the home. The children may not be able to define the event or its implications, but they are well aware that something is unsteady, that status quo is in jeopardy.

Insecurity is that indescribable feeling a child has when he doesn't know what he can hang on to if something goes wrong. Watch a small child learning to ride his first two-wheel bicycle. The one teaching him runs down the street with his hand on the back of the seat, giving encouragement and an added sense of balance. When the hand on the seat is removed, the bike rider is on his own. Everything continues as before—until the child becomes aware that the hand on the back is gone. The front wheel wobbles, and within a few feet the once-confident rider hits the ground.

What happened? Insecurity! It exploded the instant the rider became aware he was on his own.

Children need to know that there's a hand on the saddle of their lives, providing balance should anything upset their equilibrium. If they sense that the hand is missing or has become undependable, they lapse into some form of upset: a stomachache, babyish behavior reminiscent of three years earlier, aggressiveness, and other attempts at gaining attention.

The security need of a child is normally met by a reasonable amount of consistency in a home: regularity of schedule, stability of place, and normalcy of responsibilities and relationships. Whenever Dad foresees that one of these patterns must necessarily be disrupted, he should go to extra lengths to reassure his small children about what is going to happen and how they can cope with unsettled feelings and fears.


## PUBERTY

A second set of emotional stresses to children begins during preadolescence. If fathers do not sensitize themselves to these changes, they will be unequipped to cope with the "surprises" that come in their children's pubescent behavior. Reacting impulsively to situations, they will alienate their children when they should be drawing them significantly closer.

Puberty brings enormous changes in the moods and feelings of young boys and girls. Various glands are moving into operation to trigger later adult functions. It may take several years for the new hormonal secretions to be balanced. Endocrinologists tell us that early adolescents can be overwhelmed by massive "overdoses" of one hormone or another, causing high moments of exhilaration or low moments of depression.

Parents who do not easily understand the pubescent child may demand that he explain moods that he can't control, stop crying when in fact he can't fathom why he started, and be more careful when in fact his clumsiness is an equal embarrassment to him. Parents should remember that the child is probably having just as difficult a time figuring himself out as they are.

A great dad should anticipate the dynamics of puberty. He needs to carefully study the conditions and effects of puberty long before his children arrive at that stage of life. He can then take great pains to share with his children what to expect.

## PEER PRESSURE

One of the greatest stresses on our children today is the tyranny of adolescent peer pressure. It begins to touch a human being significantly somewhere about the sixth grade level, at an age of eleven or twelve years.

Peer consciousness appears to commence at the moment that boys and girls first evidence an interest in the opposite sex. My son Mark permits me to quote him on the subject: his one aim in life used to be to remain unmarried so that he could be a dolphin trainer and enjoy a monkey, a boa constrictor, and a German shepherd for pets. Since he figured girls were generally uninterested in such things, Mark always made it plain that he had no place for girls in his life.

The change of values came in one seven-day period. As if a curtain had been drawn shut on one life-style and opened dramatically on another, monkeys, boa constrictors, and German shepherds were traded for interest in A Girl.

Along with this came a new kind of friendship with boys. No longer were conversations restricted to discussions about soccer and baseball. They took on a new and vast dimension: which boy liked what girl, and which girl liked what boy.

I began to overhear long conferences on the phone about who said what about whom. It became important to dress in a special way and to make an appearance at certain functions. The opinions of the group prevailed—binding on each individual. I heard a growing tendency toward a subtle but ruthless segregation: the "ins" feeling rather self-righteous as they compared themselves favorably to the "outs."

As a father I was informed of things I must do and must not do, lest I embarrass my children in front of their peers. I might have been tempted to disregard this if I had not fortunately remembered that I had had the exact same fears, at the same age, in the same situations. I could either become impulsively frustrated by my son's new peer-oriented behavior and alienate him by abusing the system, or I could help him see it through with reasonable restraint and well-thought-out counsel.


YOUTHFUL FATIGUE

Life simply does not go on as consistently for a youngster with a tired body and mind as it does for an adult. Peak adult strength brings us a large capacity for physical and mental energy. We can go on at a hectic pace for long periods of time before we begin to show the results of fatigue. But at least three kinds of people cannot do this: old people, sick people, and children.

We discovered something about the effects of fatigue in our youngest when she went off to school. In conference, her kindergarten teacher mentioned troublesome patterns of irritability, restlessness, and "whineyness." She asked about Kristi's bedtime.

We said that although we tried to have Kristi in bed by 7:30 every evening, it was hard to meet that deadline every night. So, we admitted, bedtime tended to fluctuate.

Kristi's teacher was quite blunt with us, and we were thankful that she was. She strongly advised us that our daughter needed a consistent bedtime virtually every night of the week. There might be an occasional exception, but we could not permit an uneven schedule and expect a six-year-old to be alert and to perform well each morning.

It was painful to follow that advice. Gail had to drop out of some evening activities that I enjoyed having her attend. Sometimes I had to arrange to be at home so that Gail could meet her obligations. But Kris's bedtime became an important priority. Within days there was a noticeable difference in her schoolwork and behavior.

The frightening thing is that we could have pinned the guilt for her behavior patterns solely on her. It is conceivable that we could have fretted, scolded, and punished over a behavior that was really our fault. How often does that happen in homes?

## INNER CONFLICTS

Foresightful leadership requires a sensitivity to struggles within the human spirit of a young person. As adults, we allow ourselves a considerable amount of flexibility for our inner conflicts. We can pass off our sharp words with a quick "I'm not myself today." We expect forgiveness for our mistakes, understanding for our failures. It is easy, however, to be less charitable to children.

An impulsive father is liable to treat every action of his children with the same response. He has not taken the time to look into the circumstances and ask why the behavior is as it is. He does not allow his children the "reasonable" flexibility of days when nothing quite works. He has not sensed that there are moments when a child wonders if he is of any value as a human being, whether or not he can ever amount to anything, whether or not he can ever please anyone.

The foresightful father expects these struggles and prepares himself for the days when his offspring will pass through them. He is ready with the answers to questions when they're asked because he has prepared. But he also learns the subtle difference between force-feeding and gently offering his insight.

In contrast, the impulsive father flies off the handle every time he senses that his children are departing from the accepted way or conviction. He blames the school, bans certain friendships, and unthinkingly condemns all kinds of outside influences.

What he does, however, in addition to alienating his son or daughter, is begin to focus suspicion upon his own ability to think things through objectively. At the very time he should have been raising his credibility as a sound and practical thinker, he is lowering it and demonstrating why it might not be wise for his children to tell Dad everything they are thinking. Dad simply doesn't "understand."

FAMILY CONFLICTS

A foresightful father is watching for conflicts that arise among family members—and the resultant stress.

I discovered, for example, that we could expect conflict between the children when there were differing opinions about which TV shows to watch. When we have purchased something significant for one child and nothing for the other, we can expect that jealousy will spark conflict.

Conflicts arise for the same reason when one child has done something that receives high recognition, such as earning an award at school, playing on an athletic team, or being praised for some special thing done around the house.

If a dad watches for patterns of behavioral clash, he can be prepared for conflict and can learn how to prevent painful moments the family ought not to experience.

Not all conflict is unhealthy, of course.

Not all conflict is unavoidable, and fathers and mothers cannot feel guilty or inadequate when the best behaved children become defensive or argumentative. It happens; they are human. But when we become aware that certain types of clashes are happening with growing frequency and that they are becoming destructive to the unity of the family, then it is time to find ways to avoid the conditions in which such problems emerge.

## WHAT'S YOUR CHILD'S STRESS LEVEL?

Identify for each child the pressure or pressures that might be most relevant, putting a check in the appropriate square.

| Child: | Insecurity | Puberty | Peer Pressure | Youthful Fatigue | Inner Conflicts | Family Conflicts |
|---|---|---|---|---|---|---|
|  |  |  |  |  |  |  |
|  |  |  |  |  |  |  |
|  |  |  |  |  |  |  |
|  |  |  |  |  |  |  |

# *Implement Rules That Work*

Can a canoe turn over in the middle of a quiet, lazy river just three feet deep? Absolutely—if someone decides to stand up and wave to a friend on the shore! Rule number one, my family learned the wet way, is that one never stands in a canoe, waves violently, or shifts weight in a sudden manner. We learned a few lessons about canoeing the hard way, and it soon became obvious that we had to plot out the laws of behavior for water safety.

That's very much like what has to happen in our homes. Families need rules for living together—rules that may be few in number, but should be inviolable in observance. The man who does not believe in rules and allows his family to exist in an atmosphere of constant uncertainty will reap the result: an unstable home life in which relationships are undefined and probably exploited. He will find himself trying to demand good behavior on the strength of his own forcefulness, and he'll have to make up impromptu rules as he goes along. Any way you look at it, his home will be one step short of disaster all the time.

When I analyze our own family rules, I discover that they fall into two categories: laws and convictions. Laws are those matters of behavior that are not open to interpretation. We did not dream them up. They were given to us from the Scriptures by God himself. Laws are the unnegotiable, profound forms of behavior that every human being has to learn or face serious consequences.

Convictions, on the other hand, are those standards of conduct the family decides to maintain because they believe them to be right for them. Certain convictions or standards may differ from person to person, family to family. We should not judge another person or family because they do not share our convictions, nor should we count ourselves as superior to or more spiritual than another whose convictions are different. The important thing is that we form and submit ourselves to certain convictions we believe to be right and healthy for our style of life.


## THREE LAWS WORTH LEARNING

Let's talk about a few laws worth learning.

1. *Truthfulness.* Respect for truth is something that should be established at the very beginning of childhood.

My father placed great emphasis upon

telling the truth—whatever the consequences. In my earliest years, he made it plain that lying would be met with the severest of punishments. Truthfulness, on the other hand, would be enthusiastically affirmed.

I soon found out that he meant what he said. It was better, I learned, to own up to bad behavior than to attempt to cover it up. He had a way of finding things out, and improper behavior compounded by lying was the ultimate in family crime at our house. If such an occasion arose, he threw the book at me. I'm glad he did.

My dad did see this thing both ways, and he was equally diligent about accepting, affirming, and rewarding me when he knew I had faced the truth, even when it was painful.

By the age of five or six, truth-telling had become an automatic practice. I remember the day when the observance of this basic rule really paid off. Someone had set the underbrush on fire in an empty lot near our home. Before long the firemen arrived with their hoses and went to work. Right behind them were the police with their questions. Since I had been seen that day with matches in my hands, someone pointed the finger of suspicion at me. It didn't take long for the policeman to become quite sure I was guilty.

I remember my father taking me aside and saying, "I'm just going to ask the question once: Did you have anything to do with starting the fire?" My negative answer was all he needed. He never asked a follow-up question. He never demanded any kind of proof. He never had to. My word was sufficient.

He informed the police that I was not guilty, and they resumed their investigation. Later in the day, another boy confessed to the arson, and I learned the high value of establishing credibility.

My father had foresight. He had known there would come times when truth-telling would be absolutely essential. He had ground into me a regard for truth and the habit of facing it, no matter what the result. When the moment came in which truth was all-important, he could trust my word.

---

**☞ C H E C K P O I N T**
Can you identify the specific laws that govern your home?

---

2. *Respect.* Another basic law for family relationships is respect for those in authority—essentially one's elders and those who fill special offices in our society. There are people to whom all of us must submit: teachers, policemen, spiritual leaders, etc.

Don't confuse respect for authority with inability to disagree; there's a difference. What we are talking about is the early childhood teaching that there is no place in the home for sarcasm, ridicule, unrestrained anger, or questioning the right of those in authority over us to make judgments that will prevail.

A great dad will establish this principle early in the life of the family. He must emphasize the children's total respect for their mother, for example. He makes it plain that behavior that undermines the role of those in authority is unthinkable and will not be tolerated. If he means what he says, disrespect simply will not happen.

3. *Obedience.* A father sets obedience as a high priority in his children's lives because he knows there are potential moments when automatic obedience may be the thing that saves a life.

In the earliest years, a child should be taught to obey his parents as a reflex. The Bible makes that very plain. Obedience should never be tied to the question "why?" As a child grows older, a parent will explain his decisions more and more. But first a child must learn to obey, not because there is a reason but because it is his parents' wish.

Some parents reject this notion. To require blind obedience, they suggest, is to hinder a person's ability to make good decisions on his own. But obedience is based on the concept that the one in authority is issuing his commands for the child's good. If we are never taught to obey our parents, we will never learn how to obey God. The two understandings go hand in hand.

If obedience has been given a high priority in the earliest years, it will become less and less necessary for a parent to restrict his children through sheer command in the later years. They will have a basic order of life on which they can build independently as they mature.

There are other basic laws of family life that are inviolable, but these three seem especially significant. If basic laws—and not too many—are established, a great dad will defuse about 85 percent of the classic family explosions.

## SAMPLE CONVICTIONS

A great dad should build a second level of control: a series of understood convictions. With his wife, he establishes patterns of behavior in which the two believe and to which the family will subscribe. When crises come, there will be no need for panic if family leaders can act out of understood and well-developed convictions.

1. *Family loyalty.* In our household, we have a conviction about family loyalty—a conviction that we owe each other a certain faithfulness no matter what the situation. We may disagree energetically with one another over issues when we are at home, but when one of us is in trouble, we stick together. Our children have found this out in a multitude of ways. When they have faced an emergency at school, they know their mother and father will do their best to come to their aid.

Recently, Mark was preparing a school project that made it necessary for him to get up extremely early every morning for a week. It was an opportunity for me to share a joint hardship with him and he was impressed that I would arrange to get up and keep him company during the dark hours of a winter morning. An act of this sort establishes a conviction: that we stick together and uphold one another.

2. *Help for the hurting.* We have a conviction that our family will join together to aid people we know are in trouble. God has blessed us in many ways, and we feel compelled to share those blessings. We have set ourselves to serving other people as a family. When guests come into our home, each of us takes on the added tasks that extend hospitality. The ultimate benefit and blessing from giving is equally distributed among us all.

3. *Dating standards.* We have convictions about dating ages, dating circumstances, and times for arrival home. Gail and I carefully explained ground rules for the kids long before individual decisions had to be made. This prevented us from being arbitrary at the last minute and conveying the feeling that we were simply trying to interfere with the children's "fun."

4. *Healthy living.* I have also tried to establish an order of personal living that will help our children see the importance of healthy living. My wife and I have a conviction about the use of alcohol and tobacco,

overeating, and the misuse of money.

There are many things we could have purchased both for ourselves and for the children, but we have painfully developed the ability to say "no." While we may be able to handle some of these possessions responsibly, we are not sure that our young children can do so. It is better to practice some restraint than to splurge—and discover too late that your children can't control their materialistic desires.


## BE PREPARED WITH ALTERNATIVES

*NASA*—the space flight people—call it contingency thinking, and I think they taught us something about problem-solving.

When they set out to put a man on the moon, one of the key parts of their program was to anticipate every possible thing that could go wrong. Vast volumes were put together, detailing every potential problem and the proper response. They simply refused to be surprised.

A great dad does that. Talking with other fathers, he develops a vast catalog of experiences and proper responses. He holds strong values, reaches into his own experience, and formulates key reactions to circumstances that could arise in his home.

- Knowing that one of his kids is liable to ask to go out tonight on the spur of the moment, what will his answer be?

- Sensing that a boy has been ignoring his schoolwork, how can he plan an occasion on which they can talk it through?
- Aware that his daughter has been spending a day with some other girls who are known to have poor relationships with their parents, how will he react if she comes home and tests her parents' authority? What are the contingencies in any critical set of circumstances?

A foresightful father is always thinking one step ahead. He knows the laws and convictions that bind his family and he is prepared to enforce them.

# *Follow Four Steps to Sound Decisions*

Once on a canoe outing, I invited a couple of friends who had never steered a canoe through white water. My first mistake was to put them both in the same craft. They were overturned and soaked within three minutes.

I should have known better than to let them go it alone, but they seemed confident. I watched them trying to choose the best way to paddle the river. It seemed that when the bowman wanted to paddle right, the sternman pushed left. Instead of keeping their canoe straight in line with the current, their indecision inevitably caused them to drift sideways. In such circumstances it's just a matter of minutes if the river is in a vengeful mood. It was, and they were in the water the first time they went over a ledge sideways.

When a great dad looks downriver in the life of his family, he has to be prepared to make good decisions. And good decisions rely on a sound decision-making process.

STEP ONE: CONSIDER THE DATA
The first thing I have to consider is the personal history and present condition of my child. Since every child is different, each decision is going to be unique. I must never allow myself to fall into the trap of premature decisions or conclusions based on inadequate data. This is an important principle when a child asks permission for an event, deserves punishment for an offense, or presents a problem for solution.

I watched a man use this principle one year at a family camp. While we were visiting together, his wife came to tell him that she strongly suspected their six-year-old had taken fifty cents out of her billfold.

When she had thought back through the morning's activities, it dawned on her that he had carefully plotted the crime, telling her to wait for him on the path while he returned to their room for something he needed. He apparently used that moment to empty his mother's wallet. When confronted, he had denied any knowledge of the missing coins. Now it appeared that stealing was compounded by lying.

The average father probably would have found the child and badgered him into a confession. The punishment would have been harsh, and the matter ended as a sick memory for all involved.

But I watched my friend think the matter through before he did anything. The three of us talked for several minutes, trying to discern why a child who had never stolen before would do so on this occasion.

Stealing is a serious offense, but it is often important to know why it occurred. Were there conditions that prompted it? Were there ways it could have been prevented? We must also ask about the tempting conditions that existed when we deal with the mistakes of our children.

My friend did just that. He learned from our conversation that most of the children in the family camp, with the exception of his son, had received allowances from their parents to spend at the camp store. The boy had been deeply hurt as he saw his camp friends purchase candy and other items while he was unable to do so.

When he had asked for money, his parents had refused, supposing that it was unnecessary. Thus they had created a condition in which stealing became an overwhelming temptation. The sin was his, but the context of the sin was shared.

The boy's father took this information into account when he confronted his son with what he knew. He said he had become aware that other children had money and were spending it, that he had made a mistake in not allowing his son to have some spending money, and that he could see why one might be tempted to take a few coins from his mother's wallet. Could this have been the case?

When the child saw that his father understood the situation even more clearly than he did, he confessed that he had indeed stolen the fifty cents.

Punishment was severe, but the conversation that surrounded the situation was salted with the admission that the parents had also made a mistake. The father settled on an allowance after the offense had been confessed and paid for, and life was resumed in an atmosphere of forgiveness and restoration.

We must know the context of the matter and the background of the person involved if we are going to make good decisions concerning the affairs of our children. Each child must be evaluated on the basis of his particular needs and weaknesses. A great dad does not make a decision until he knows all of this.

## STEP TWO: WEIGH LONG-TERM EFFECTS

Involve the future tense. What is the long-term growth dimension of the decision at hand? A father is not a baby-sitter; he is part of the process in which a human being is being sculptured. The chiseling process may at times be painful; sometimes it may appear to be quite out of perspective. But the sculptor knows what he is creating; therefore, he is patient and deliberate. His work is based on the future.

I don't expect my children to see the logic of everything that I ask of them. They tend to think only of the present. But I try to think of the future and where a particular choice is going to take them.

As a prep school student, I had the privilege of running track and cross-country for Mr. Marvin Goldberg of the Stony Brook School. Goldberg believed that all athletics were aimed at the development of character and integrity in the human experience. Year after year, he turned out championship teams and individuals. But more important, he turned out men whose adult lives were marked by many of the experiences he created for them on the track.

I remember my decision to quit the cross-country team in my senior year so I could, as I wrote to him during the summer, "enjoy a few months of fun before I graduated." Cross-country—running ten and fifteen miles a day, five miles in competition—was painful, unpleasant, and too demanding, I told him.

Marvin Goldberg's written response was a milestone in my life. He informed me that as I grew older, many matters of life would be "painful, unpleasant, and too demanding." Sooner or later I would develop a pattern of response to such situations. I could develop the habit of quitting—or I could learn to bear the pain and inconvenience, doing the hard things for the good of those about me. Dropping out of cross-country might set in motion a pattern of escape that would follow me for the rest of my life. But to return and master something I didn't want to do—and to do it for the good of the team—would be to exercise a healthier pattern of response.

I followed that advice, and two decades later, Marvin Goldberg's character lesson still follows me every day. Having run cross-country—painfully and unenjoyably—I have faced almost every inconvenient situation ever since with the mental determination that began those early days on the running course: "I did it then; I can do it again!"

The world in which our children live appeals almost solely to the present: own this, do that, be what your friends want. A father is one of the only significant people in a child's life who will take the future into account. Thus, his decisions must always relate to what they are becoming. His view is long-range.

## STEP THREE: THINK OF OTHER PEOPLE

A third significant key to decision-making is taking into account the effects of our children's wishes on other people.

A great dad begins in the earliest years to point out to his children—in the words of poet John Donne—that no man is an island. Everything we say, do, or have affects someone else. Our decisions, our exercise of personal rights, the pursuit of our goals cannot be conducted in a relational vacuum.

Watch children at play in the neighborhood. You will note that some are cruel with their words—criticizing and bullying others into submission, oblivious to the effect on the victim's self-esteem. When Mark first wore braces on his teeth, some of his friends enjoyed kidding him about it—until they suddenly had to have the silver in their mouths.

The person who dominates people, exploits them, or uses them for his own purposes in business or community politics is often a product of a home where life was never evaluated on the basis of good for others. Children can be taught at a very early age to think of others. It is never too early to start or too late to get busy.


## STEP FOUR: MAKE EXCEPTIONS

In making good decisions, we also must be able to determine appropriate exceptions. Are we flexible enough to let out the rope on occasion to test our children? Will we allow them to make some of their own decisions? A great dad follows laws and convictions. But he is not rigid.

Recently a movie came to our community and all of my son's friends were going to see it. The social pressure was on, and everyone was talking about having seen the film or going to see it. The rating on the film violated our family's convictions, and the normal decision would have been to say, "No way!"

Gail and I talked for some time about this decision. We felt uneasy about following the regular course. We sensed a confusion of priorities and situations. It seemed to be a time for an exception. We agreed that out of this situation might come a learning experience.

I went to Mark and suggested a solution. We would go to see the film together so we could talk about it when it was over. He agreed and was quite excited. A few days later we went. It was among the better decisions Gail and I have made.

Mark was repelled by the film. The violence shocked him, and he had a hard time getting to sleep that evening. But in the process of talking the film through, he came to understand why our family had drawn a line—a conviction—in the matter of movies. A valuable year has passed now in which we have never been asked for permission to attend anything but a G-rated film.

Our children know of our convictions about the use of tobacco. But since a large percentage of our population chooses to ignore the obvious facts linking smoking to cancer, they cannot help but become curious about what the experience is that draws people to such a habit. Both their mother and I had told Mark and Kris that they were welcome to try smoking a cigarette anytime they wished to satisfy their curiosity—as long as they would do it in our presence.

The time came when they asked. It was the moment for an exception. I went to the store and bought the smelliest unfiltered cigarettes I could find.

On a camping trip we opened the pack and allowed them to light a cigarette. At first they laughed at the ease with which they could puff and blow out the smoke. Then I suggested that they inhale.

Once was enough. We had two green-faced children. The rest of the package was trashed. Our children have resolved the smoking problem for at least a few years until they have to make their own adult decisions.

Exceptions cannot be made on every issue of conviction. Exceptions can never be made on the laws of God. But there are times when a father must be sensitive enough to know that he must loosen the lines and give opportunity for experiment and experience.

## IS THERE A PRICE TO PAY?

We've all heard the story of some person who is offered a chance to purchase a few shares in a tiny company. By investing the paltry sum of a few hundred dollars, he can gain possession of several dozen company shares.

But the price is too high, the potential investor says; the risk is too great. So he passes up the opportunity.

What about the company? Its idea catches fire, and after a short struggle, it begins to sell products. Before one knows what has happened, the little company that started on a shoestring is grossing millions in annual income.

Someone always computes what the investor who originally turned down an opportunity to buy shares could have been worth—perhaps millions of dollars. But he isn't! When the opportunity was embryonic, the price was too high.

Like a fledgling company, a young child seems so small, nondescript, and even easy to handle with minimum concern. It is simple for a young father to reason that there are more important things demanding his time and energy: advanced degrees, a climb up the corporate ladder, and lots of fun while one is still young.

What the imperceptive father does not see is that the time to make family investments is when the child is young. Big returns never happen in the future unless sizable investments are made in the present.

Is there a price to pay for being a great dad? Unquestionably! But there is no greater opportunity.

**MY INVESTMENT**
For me, the price of being a great dad is

_______________________________________________

_______________________________________________

_______________________________________________

I am willing to pay this price! I deliberately set as one of my life's highest priorities the creation of conditions in my home that will stimulate my children to grow to their full potential.

_________________________________     _____________
Signature                            Date

*About the Author*

GORDON MACDONALD is president of Inter-Varsity Christian Fellowship-USA and former senior minister of Grace Chapel in Lexington, Massachusetts. He is the author of several books, including *Ordering Your Private World* (Nelson) and *Magnificent Marriage* (Tyndale). He and his wife Gail live in Middleton, Wisconsin.

- *The Perfect Way to Lose Weight* by Charles T. Kuntzleman and Daniel V. Runyon. Anyone can lose fat—and keep it off permanently. This tested program, developed by a leading physical fitness expert, shows how. 72-4935-9 $2.25.

- *Strange Cults in America* by Bob Larson. An easy-reading update of six well-known cults: the Unification Church, Scientology, The Way International, Rajneesh, Children of God, and Transcendental Meditation. 72-6675-X $2.25.

- *Temper Your Child's Tantrums* by Dr. James Dobson. You don't need to feel frustrated as a parent. The celebrated author and "Focus on the Family" radio host wants to give you the keys to firm, but loving, discipline in your home. 72-6994-5 $2.25.

- *When the Doctor Says, "It's Cancer"* by Mary Beth Moster. Cancer will strike approximately three out of four American families. Find out how to cope when you or someone you love hears this diagnosis. 72-7981-9 $2.25.

- *When Your Friend Needs You* by Paul Welter. Do you know what to say when a friend comes to you for help? Here's how to express your care in an effective way. 72-7998-3 $2.25.